After the Altar Call

By Arnold Reasons

Acknowledgements & Encouragement for the Reader

Special thanks to my amazing team who helped make this possible. It wouldn't have been possible without you.

And to the reader: this book was several years in the making. After many starts and stops, we finally got it over the line. Be encouraged to know that there's no condemnation if you fail to hit your goals first time (second, third, fourth etc!). Pick yourself up and keep on going. This race is a marathon, not a sprint.

after the altar call | reasontobehold.com

Introduction

Around the end of 2008, I finally raised the white flag
and surrendered to God. I'd mostly grown up in and
around the church, so the lingo and clichés were second
nature to me. I quickly answered questions like "how are
you?" with empty routine responses rather than
authenticity. But in the midst of all the inauthentic traits
and traditions I'd adopted as my own, there was a heavy
yearning to go deeper with God.

My hunger for more with God was starkly challenged by
my destructive relationship with sin. Even though I'd
turned my back on a number of the sins I'd once been so
well acquainted with, I found myself ping-ponging
between victory and defeat. I desperately wanted to
escape the chains that seemed to chase and arrest me
from time-to-time. It was exhausting. It was
discouraging. And it dampened my flames of hope,
causing me to question whether I would ever truly
become victorious over these inescapable evils.

2

What I've just described is just one of many experiences I've had since becoming a Christian. Even after my conversion, sin still seemed to have an aggressive hold over me. Even though I was still being transformed daily, there were certain things that didn't sit right with me at all. There were clear disconnects from what I was reading in the scriptures and what I was experiencing in my life. The following verses highlighted this:

"Do not let sin control the way you live; do not give in to sinful desires. Do not let any part of your body become an instrument of evil to serve sin. Instead, give yourselves completely to God, for you were dead, but now you have new life. So use your whole body as an instrument to do what is right for the glory of God. Sin is no longer your master, for you no longer live under the requirements of the law. Instead, you live under the freedom of God's grace" (Romans 6:12-14 NLT).

I read verses like these, and couldn't seem to understand why I felt so far from a life free from sin. Despite the depth of *this* frustration, there was more to what troubled my mind…

I was also disturbed by how noticeably short my journey of faith seemed to fall. I knew I was a child of God, the Creator and King. But I struggled to walk completely full of faith when faced by the trials of life. In the earlier days of my Christianity, there were moments of radical, child-like faith. Times when I would believe that *anything* was possible with God. But as I grew older, I became *"rational"*. By doing so, I sold myself far short of what God has made available to His children.

Many of you can probably identify with the frustrations above. Constantly being dominated by sin on some level and not walking in the freedom which Christ came to give (see Galatians 5:1). Feeling the noticeable disconnect from what you read in the scriptures and what you see in your life. These frustrations and disconnects cause for many to settle for a mediocre *form* of Christianity. This is a result of Satan's deceit, and it

4

produces half-baked believers who don't seem any different than morally decent unbelievers.

This book contains a number of key insights I wish somebody had given to me after my conversion. It aims to equip the reader with an understanding of the restored God-nature, and the resulting implications this *should* have on the daily lives of God's children. God has called us into a deeply intimate relationship with Him. This was for *much more* than life insurance after death. This book aims to reveal *the more* that exists.

Chapter 1: Made in the image of God

When God decided to make man, He based the blueprint on Himself. Take a look at the following verses:

*"Then God said, "Let us make man **in our image, after our likeness**. And let them have dominion over the fish of the sea and over the birds of the heavens and over the livestock and over all the earth and over every creeping thing that creeps on the earth." So God created man in his own image, in the image of God he created him; male and female he created them. And God blessed them. And God said to them, "Be fruitful and multiply and fill the earth and subdue it, and have dominion over the fish of the sea and over the birds of the heavens and over every living thing that moves on the earth""* (Genesis 1:26-28).

Distorting the image of God

God created us to be His children and representatives on earth. We were made with His nature, meaning we were designed to reflect His attributes and ways on earth (this will be referred to as the 'God-nature' throughout). This

6

was much more than just a religious devotion, and more accurately described a way of living. Our God-nature permeated *all* areas of life, including things like:

- Our God-given mandate to rule over *all* of creation and the earth (Genesis 1:26)
- Our creative ability to name things that were once nameless (Genesis 2:19-20)
- Our godly work ethic which needed no managerial oversight (Genesis 2:15)

Reflecting God's nature here on earth, man once lived in perfect harmony with God's creative order. It's no wonder that shortly after creating and commissioning man, God saw all that He'd made and said it was very good! (Genesis 1:31). Sadly, man rebelled against God's created order, seeking to go after his *own* way. Man defied God's command to not eat from the forbidden tree (see Genesis 3). In so doing, man distorted the identity and God-nature he was created with. He no longer *looked* and *behaved* the way he was designed to. Instead, he rebelliously began to forge a new, sinful nature.

7

Since the fall, the sinful nature of man has increasingly evolved, resulting in increased wickedness across the earth. The departure from our God-nature has also affected the way we relate to creation. I don't know about you, but I can't remember a time when I stroked the mane of a lion, firmly confident that I had dominion over it. Whilst this isn't the measuring stick, it's a stark reminder of the gap between God's original design and our day-to-day experiences because of sin.

Our nature before the fall

Taking a look at Genesis, we can learn a few more key things about what life as a child of God looked like before the fall. Consider the following examples:

1. Naked and unashamed

Adam and Eve were both naked, but they weren't ashamed (Genesis 2:25). They were totally content and free from insecurities, unconcerned about the opinions of others. They were confident that God had made them

8

perfectly, lacking in nothing. This attitude comes from focussing on *God* and trusting in *His* power at work within. Paul demonstrated this same attitude after his conversion. Despite his recognition of his own unworthiness to be called an Apostle (in light of his sinful past), Paul didn't wallow in self-pity and misery. He focused on God and His work within him, boldly declaring:

"But by the grace of God I am what I am, and his grace toward me was not in vain. On the contrary, I worked harder than any of them [the apostles], though it was not I, but the grace of God that is with me" (1 Corinthians 15:9-10).

2. Confident in God's wisdom

When God placed Adam and Eve in the Garden of Eden, He gave them the freedom to eat from a *huge* range of trees. Of all the various trees God had created, He only marked one as not to be eaten from, letting Adam know the consequences of rebellion (Genesis 2:15-17). Adam and Eve had no reason to question this, but happily trusted in God's wisdom. That is, until they desired to be wise in their own eyes, and gave in to the rebellious advances of the serpent (see Genesis 3:6). This isn't something exclusive to Adam and Eve, as we've all rebelled against God's wisdom on how we ought to live, going after our own version of "wisdom" (see Romans 3:23 and 1 John 1:8). Interestingly, the book of Proverbs instructs us on a point that is very relevant to this:

"Trust in the Lord with all your heart, and do not lean on your own understanding. In all your ways acknowledge him, and he will make straight your paths. Be not wise in your own eyes; fear the Lord, and turn away from evil" (Proverbs 3:5-7).

3. Dependant on God as the Provider

God placed Adam in the Garden of Eden with all that he needed to sustain him (see Genesis 2:8-15). Before the fall, we don't see Adam or Eve wanting for anything, or trying to meet a need outside of God's provision. In fact, before Adam even *knew* he had a need for companionship, God already met the need by creating Eve (see Genesis 2:18-22 and Matthew 6:8). But their attitude changed when the serpent deceived them into thinking God had somehow sold them short. They stopped believing that God had *already* provided *all* that they needed. They also stopped believing that God would meet their needs *long* before *they* ever *realised* their needs.

Understanding the problem

Since the fall, there's been a departure from what it looks like to be a child of God. A departure from accurately reflecting God's attributes and ways on earth, no longer looking and behaving exactly like our Father. This is a departure from our original design. It's a departure from our *God-nature*.

The consequences stem deep and affect *all* areas of life. Man is no longer naked and unashamed, he no longer relies solely on God's wisdom and he's grown callous to

11

after the altar call | reasontobehold.com

any central dependence on God. This begins to paint the picture of how far we've come from God's original design and identity for mankind. And this is the heart of where our problem lies.

In the chapter that follows, we'll start to look at the bridge between God's design and the presently distant experience of mankind. By the end of this book, my prayer is that you'll confidently walk over this bridge, perfectly walking in the fullness of our God-nature, which was restored through salvation. Who knows, maybe someday you'll stroke the mane of a lion, as a result of the transformation that this book will spark in you :-).

12

Reflection and application

1. What would life look like if we all reflected God's character, personality and nature on Earth?

_____

_____

_____

_____

_____

_____

_____

_____

2. We now live in a fallen world where most of humanity doesn't reflect God's heart, character and nature. What are some of the consequences of this that we can see in the world we live in today?

_____

_____

_____

_____

_____

_____

_____

3. Have I consciously decided to surrender to God
    and learn from His nature and ways, rather than
    living life on my own terms? If not, what's
    holding me back? If yes, am I still following
    through on that decision?

    _____

    _____

    _____

    _____

    _____

    _____

    _____

4. While we might not be able to walk around naked in today's society, in what ways can we be naked and unashamed, before God and with each other?

_____

_____

_____

_____

_____

_____

_____

5. Information has never been more abundant and
more easily accessible than it is today. How does
the availability of so much information, good or
bad, affect our reliance on the wisdom of God?

_____

_____

_____

_____

_____

_____

_____

6. Retirement funds, savings accounts, investment portfolios etc are good things. Thinking about them in the context of this chapter, can these 'good' things sometimes take us away from depending entirely on God as Adam and Eve did? If so, how can we correct that?

_____

_____

_____

_____

_____

_____

_____

Chapter 2 – A bridge for the chasm

From the last chapter, we explored the departure of man from what it means to be made in the image of God. How since the fall, he stopped reflecting and living out his God-nature. Because of sin, man no longer expresses God's attributes and ways throughout the various areas of life. Through sin, man went after his own way, forging a new sinful nature. This demonstrates the problem that all of mankind has faced since the fall in the Garden of Eden. But God didn't leave us to remain in our fallen state.

Between then and now, God gave His law through Moses, to show us the true extent of our fallen state and guilt (see Romans 3:19-20, Romans 7:7, Galatians 3:19-26). As a result of the law, we're all without excuse. We're all guilty and deserving of eternal punishment for rebelling against our Father, and choosing to stray after our *own* way (Isaiah 53:6, Psalm 53:2-3). God's desire has and always will be that we'd all turn from our wicked rebellion and be saved from the eternal judgement that we deserve (see 1 Timothy 2:1-4, 2 Peter 3:9, Ezekiel 33:11). Thus, He sent Jesus Christ into the world to be a living example of how we ought to live. He then died on the cross, taking the punishment that each of us deserved for our rebellion against God (see Matthew 20:28, Romans 3:23-26, Isaiah 53:5, Romans 6:23). He resurrected three days later, fulfilling what he told the disciples (see Matthew 16:21, Matthew 17:22-23, Matthew 20:17-19, Matthew 26:31-32). He confirmed His identity as the promised Saviour by fulfilling all of the ancient prophecies. Studies have shown that the chances of one man fulfilling even just *eight* of these prophecies is 1 in 10,000,000,000,000,000,000,000,000,000 (http://www.goodnewsdispatch.org/math.html). The effect of His finished work is that those who return to God, can receive the free gift of eternal life and escape the punishment they deserve (Ephesians 2:8-9, Romans 6:23, Isaiah 44:22, John 3:18, John 3:36, John 6:40 and Romans 5:6-9). But is this *all* there is to this Christian gospel message? A get-out-of-hell-free card and nothing more? Far from it. As great a gift as this already is, at the cross, Jesus paid for much more.

Let's take a look at what Peter had to say about what was accomplished on the cross:

"[Jesus]...bore our sins in his body on the tree, that we might die to sin and live to righteousness. By his wounds you have been healed. For you were straying like sheep, but have now returned to the Shepherd and Overseer of your souls" (1 Peter 2:24-25).

Shortly after my conversion, I became legalistic, demanding perfection from others despite my own sin. When I began learning of our salvation by grace through faith (see Ephesians 2:8-9, Romans 3:23-25, Romans 3:20, Galatians 2:16), I went to another extreme. I focussed purely on forgiveness from sin (past, present and future), and overlooked the rest of what Christ purchased for us. There are three key things that I've now realised stem from the cross. *Grace, mercy and power.* Let's take a look at these in turn.

21

Grace

Grace speaks of the unmerited favour of God. It's the kindness that God expresses to *all of mankind*, even though man has done nothing to deserve it. In the context of salvation, God has expressed His kindness by offering a way to be saved from judgement, without man having done anything to earn it. But there's something that makes this act of grace mind-boggling and far more valuable than we've sometimes reduced it to. Consider this.

If you were a multi-millionaire, and your best friend randomly gave you £50, this could be seen as a gift of grace. You didn't actually do anything to deserve it, your friend just gave it to you out of the kindness of their heart. Whilst I'm sure many of us would receive this gift happily, the money itself wouldn't really make much of a difference to you. I mean, you're a *multi-millionaire*. You could blow your nose on a £50 note without a care in the world. You're *already* rich as it is, so £50 doesn't exactly change your life.

22

But what if we changed the scenario a little; you're on your deathbed, desperately in need of a heart transplant. There are no donors available, so you're on a sure path to death. You're unconscious and on life-support, totally unaware of what's going on. Just when all hope seemed lost, a stranger heard about your plight. He was in great health and his heart was a perfect substitute for yours. Moved by compassion for your situation, he contacted the hospital and did what nobody expected. He agreed to give his life, so that you could have his heart and live. Imagine waking up from unconsciousness, to be told that this is what somebody did for you. It's a gift of grace not to be sniffed at, especially because of how much of a difference it makes to you. This gift of grace is something that you *couldn't* do *anything* to earn. And its value is *far beyond measure.*

This second scenario parallels what Jesus did on the cross. We were dead in our sins, deserving of death, yet He showed us His love, kindness and compassion by giving us the undeserved gift of *eternal* life (see Romans

23

5:6-9, John 3:16-18, John 15:13). In fact, we *couldn't* do anything to deserve it, since we were already condemned to eternal punishment because of our sins (see Romans 6:23). And this is all a demonstration of God's grace. Godly grace is nothing short of a **miracle** - *and this is what far too many of us miss*. Because we miss the miracle of grace, we *cheapen its power*. We misrepresent it as *just* a get-out-of-hell-free card. We *strip it of its power* to free us from the chains of sin, and to *empower* us to walk out the restored God-nature.

Sadly, the good news of Jesus and His sacrifice is often devalued, with many of us treating His gift like the first scenario. If we don't see the *real* desperation of our situation, then we won't come *anywhere* close to valuing the gospel as we should. Nor will we come to walk in the fullness of our restored God-nature, which overcomes sin and temptation, and allows us to walk and live supernaturally through faith.

Mercy

While grace is about us miraculously receiving something we had no ability to earn or deserve, mercy is centred on compassion. Compassion that expresses *"...kindness or good will toward the miserable and afflicted, joined with a desire to relieve them"* (taken from Strong's #G1656 Thayer's Greek Lexicon). Just carrying out a quick search on the New Testament shows us how common it was for people who were noticeably afflicted to ask Jesus to have mercy on them. A few examples are the two blind men (Matthew 9:27-31), the woman whose daughter was oppressed (Matthew 15:22-28), the man whose son was demon possessed (Matthew 17:14-19) and another two blind men (Matthew 20:30-34).

In the context of salvation, God saw us in our miserable and afflicted state of sin, with a sentence of eternal punishment hanging over our heads. God then demonstrated mercy by choosing to relieve us of our plight, offering eternal life and *invaluably* more (see

25

Ephesians 2:1-7). But like grace, mercy holds no value to the person who doesn't recognise their state of affliction. If you don't recognise the *true* desperation of your state, you'll fail to truly understand the weight and *value* of God's grace and mercy towards mankind (see, for example, Luke 18:9-14).

Power

Let's take a look at the following verses of scriptures, and take a few moments to really consider what they mean:

"If the Spirit of him who raised Jesus from the dead dwells in you, he who raised Christ Jesus from the dead will also give life to your mortal bodies through his Spirit who dwells in you. So then brothers, we are debtors, not to the flesh, to live according to the flesh. For if you live according to the flesh you will die, but if by the Spirit you put to death the deeds of the body, you will live" (Romans 8:11-13).

26

"So Jesus said to the Jews who had believed him, "If you abide in my word, you are truly my disciples, and you will know the truth, and the truth will set you free." They answered him, "We are offspring of Abraham and have never been enslaved to anyone. How is it that you say, 'You will become free'?" Jesus answered them, "Truly, truly, I say to you, everyone who practices sin is a slave to sin. The slave does not remain in the house forever; the son remains forever. So if the Son sets you free, you will be free indeed" (John 8:31-36).

"For freedom Christ has set us free; stand firm therefore, and do not submit again to a yoke of slavery" (Galatians 5:1).

"What then? Are we to sin because we are not under the law but under grace? By no means! Do you not know that if you present yourselves to anyone as obedient slaves, you are slaves of the one whom you obey, either of sin, which leads to death, or of obedience, which leads to righteousness? But thanks be to God, that you who were once slaves of sin have become obedient from the

27

heart to the standard of teaching to which you were
committed, and having been set free from sin, have
become slaves of righteousness. I am speaking in human
terms, because of your natural limitations. For just as
you once presented your members [or parts of your
body] as slaves to impurity and to lawlessness leading to
more lawlessness, so now present your members [or
body parts] as slaves to righteousness leading to
sanctification... But now that you have been set free
from sin and have become slaves of God, the fruit you
get leads to sanctification and its end, eternal life"
(Romans 6:15-19, 6:22).

Before the cross, we were slaves to our sin nature. We
were unable to keep ourselves from constantly yielding
to the passions of our flesh, and the patterns of this world
(see Ephesians 2:1-3, Colossians 1:21-23, Ephesians
2:11-12). After the cross, as believers, we've been set
free from the chains that this old nature had over us,
giving us the **power to say no**! (Romans 6:17-18,
Romans 6:22, Romans 8:1-2. See also Luke 4:16-21).
Sin will no longer have *any* rule over us as believers, as

we're no longer bound to our old sinful nature (Romans 6:12-14). We were reborn with a new nature and identity (2 Corinthians 5:17). This nature and identity is the God-nature we were originally created with! This is truly something to be excited about, because it changes *everything*.

Grace, Mercy and Power

How do grace, mercy and power come together in relation to the cross? Mercy implies that the one being shown mercy is afflicted. The bondage of the sinful nature and its ensnaring power is the affliction of mankind. Man is enslaved by this disease and its deadly consequences, putting him on the path to eternal destruction. Knowing that man had no means to purchase his freedom, God, moved by compassion (*mercy*), took the punishment that man deserved, purchasing his freedom from sin and death (*grace*). This freedom means that the prison doors have been *burst wide open*. Man can now walk out *no longer bound* by the chains that his old sinful nature once had on him. He no longer has to be

29

looped in a constant cycle of yielding to the sinful nature, but can now stand firm according to his new identity and the restored God-nature! (*power*)

An important caveat

Since we're discussing sin and man's power to say no, it becomes important to outline some underlying truths. Whilst man now has the power to say no to sin, his performance and good works *do not* justify him before God (see Ephesians 2:8-9 and Romans 3:20). The bible makes it clear that *if* a believer sins, we have an advocate - Jesus Christ, who paid the price for *all* of our sins (1 John 2:1-2). It also makes it clear that if we confess our sins, He is faithful and just to forgive us (1 John 1:9). Given the context of these verses, as well as all that we've discussed in this chapter, the standard for a Christian isn't to go on sinning. We're urged *not* to sin, but given provision for any occasions in which we do sin (1 John 2:1). This is the standard we're called to - one which strives and presses on to increasingly walk out the full God-nature we have been restored to by God. After all, the grace of God takes us on a lifelong journey of teaching and growth. Teaching us to increasingly renounce ungodliness and worldly passions, living self-controlled, upright and godly lives (see Titus 2:11-12).

Eternal life is a free gift from God, resulting from His grace and mercy toward mankind. As a result of God's gift, and the freedom that it brings, the first response of man is to *love* God. Recognising the weight of our hopeless plight without the cross, our second response should be nothing short of a desire to live for Him. Not under compulsion, but from a genuine place of love and gratitude.

The second response of man is a natural outworking of the first. And that's what we'll be looking at in the next chapter.

Reflection and application

1. The law was given to show us the true extent of
   our fallen state, but we don't always actively
   recognise this. What do you think full recognition
   of what the law is and means for mankind should
   look like? (Luke 5:8 & Isaiah 6:5 are great
   starting points).

   _____

   _____

   _____

   _____

   _____

   _____

2. It's easy to focus on the laws you don't break and become self-righteous, legalistic and/or critical of others. How can an understanding of what Grace really is prevent us from these errors?

_____

_____

_____

_____

_____

_____

_____

3. The other extreme of this conversation is to fall into the deception that Grace means we can go on sinning without consequence. How does the wisdom and power of God (now also available to us) help us to avoid this erroneous concept?

_____

_____

_____

_____

_____

_____

4. The Concepts of God's mercy, His grace and His
   power are often treated and thought of in
   isolation alone. What are the benefits and
   drawbacks of doing so (if any)?

_____

_____

_____

_____

_____

_____

_____

5. What would a person living with a great understanding of God's mercy, grace, and power look like? Does your life look like this? If not, how can you apply the lessons in this chapter to help you get there?

_____

_____

_____

_____

_____

_____

_____

Chapter 3 – Be holy, for He is holy

If the title of this chapter is taken in isolation, it will excite those who believe eternal life is simply a reward for good works, and frustrate those who believe that man can't have victory over sin on this side of eternity. Don't let either of these extremes derail you from the journey we've been on so far. In this chapter, we'll take a look at holiness and how the power discussed in chapter two empowers us to walk in holiness.

Let's consider the following verses:

"As obedient children, do not be conformed to the passions of your former ignorance, but as he who called you is holy, you also be holy in all your conduct, since it is written, "You shall be holy, for I am holy"" (1 Peter 1:14-16).

Work out what God has worked in...

We're instructed as *children*; those with young and malleable minds in need of *complete* training. Childhood is a journey of *constant learning and growing*, expected to end at the next stage of maturity. The same is true of life after our conversion. We surrender to God and experience a spiritual *re-birth* (John 3:1-14). We enter as new-born babies in need of training (1 Peter 2:2, Matthew 18:1-4), with the expectation that we would go on to become fully mature. It was for this reason that God gave the roles of apostles, prophets, evangelists, pastors and teachers – so that we would go from being children when we first enter in, to becoming mature, *exactly* like Jesus, *fully* living out the God-nature that was restored in us at conversion (Ephesians 4:11-16).

Between childhood and full maturity, there's a great deal of training, learning and growth needed. This takes place primarily in our minds, as we learn how to think, reason and discern as wise and mature spiritual adults (Hebrew 5:14). Our minds need to be washed and rewired by

38

God's truth, following His way rather than the patterns of this world (Romans 12:2). The key to making this process progressive rather than stagnant is *intentional obedience.* We intentionally obey, *not* in order to be accepted by God – but *because* we **know** we've *already* been accepted by Him.

If you tell a child to stay away from fire because it will burn them, the child has two choices:

1. Listen to what they've heard, and benefit from the safety it provides.

2. Ignore what they've heard, and learn the pain of being burnt through their experiences.

When our Father tells us not to go back to our former passions (1 Peter 1:14-16), we're faced with the same two options. We can choose to learn by hearing His instruction and *trusting* (faith) in His wisdom. Alternatively, we can choose to learn the hard way by experiencing the pain of getting burnt.

Our restored God-nature doesn't work on autopilot – it requires *intentional* input from us. Faith without works is dead, beliefs with no supporting action achieve nothing (see James 2:14-26). It's God who *empowers* you to walk out the restored God-nature (see Ezekiel 36:22-27, Philippians 2:12-13). But you have to go from just *saying* you believe this, to *walking* it out in your daily living.

We saw in the previous chapter that the grace of God takes us on a lifelong journey. It *teaches* us to renounce ungodliness and worldly passions. It teaches us to live self-controlled, upright and godly lives (Titus 2:11-12). *Practically* speaking, what does that look like? God's unmerited favour (grace) is seen through His promise of the gift of eternal life to His children, *despite* the eternal punishment *deserved* for our offences against Him. This…enables us…to *breathe*. We're no longer caught up trying to *earn* eternal life, because we *know* we're secure as a result of His promise.

God's grace *frees* us from the exhausting exercise of *trying* to measure up in our own strength, but *always* coming short (Isaiah 64:6). The grace of God is *life-giving* and *full of freedom*! And it takes away the burden of condemnation because His acceptance is *not* based on our performance!

God's grace *liberates* us from the weight of *hopelessness* that comes from *failing* to follow His instructions (Romans 8:1). When we realise that His choice to save and adopt us had nothing to do with our performance (Ephesians 2:8-10), it gives us *good* reasons to trust in His Wisdom above our own. It shows us that He has no ulterior motive behind the instructions He gives us. The only motivation is *love*. It's *because* of His love that God entered this broken world to pay the price for our redemption (John 3:16). He found us, put us on His shoulders and took us away from destruction (Luke 15:4-7). He also gave us His instructions so we could live life in abundance (John 10:10).

41

Without the grace of God, it would be *impossible* for us to *ever* have eternal life (Romans 3:20, Romans 8:3-4, Isaiah 64:6, Galatians 2:16). This perfectly explains why God's grace is the *central* thing that makes *possible* what was otherwise *impossible*. The grace of God is like an inexhaustible battery that gives a *lifeless* car the *ability* to start-up and get in motion. *This* is what God's grace is to *us* as His children – it raises us up from our dead and lifeless state, and *enables* us to *walk in a manner worthy of our calling* (Romans 6:4-14, Ephesians 4:1).

Putting a working car battery under the bonnet doesn't make the car start-up and drive itself. The battery only makes a difference if it's *engaged* by the driver. Likewise, the degree to which we live out our restored God-nature will be dependent on how much we intentionally connect to His grace and the freedom it provides. This is where *intentional obedience* is key.

For the person unconsciously seeking to *earn* God's approval and eternal life; trying to live up to God's standards will only *highlight* their sin and bring hopelessness. That's why the law was given – to *expose* the sin in man, and make clear his *need* for salvation (Romans 3:20). But for the person who has *received* the undeserved gift of eternal life; intentional obedience is not a matter of approval and acceptance, since they already have this. For them, it's about walking out the restored God-nature - living out the reborn identity that was birthed at their conversion. It is for this reason that the following verses don't *condemn* us as children of God, but *guide* us according to our *new* nature:

*"Now this I say and testify in the Lord, that **you must no longer walk as the Gentiles do, in the futility of their minds**. They are darkened in their understanding, alienated from the life of God because of the ignorance that is in them, due to their hardness of heart. They have become callous and have given themselves up to sensuality, greedy to practice every kind of impurity. **But that is not the way you learned Christ!** — assuming that you have heard about him and were taught in him, as the truth is in Jesus, to **put off your old self, which belongs to your former manner of life and is corrupt through***

deceitful desires, and to be renewed in the spirit of your minds, and to put on the new self, created after the likeness of God in true righteousness and holiness" *(Ephesians 4:17-24 – see also verses 25-32)*

Holiness?

Now let's talk about "holiness". Let's put aside the connotations this word may already have in our minds, and let's actually dig into the root meaning.

Strong's Concordance defines the word 'holy' (as used in 1 Peter 1:14-16) as: *set apart by (or for) God or sacred.* Being set apart, in this context, paints the picture of being *different* from what is common. Sacred, in this definition, suggests some form of *dedication to God.* So ultimately, we are different from the world because of our dedication to God. Our dedication here isn't *defined* by our earthly performance – things like, showing up for Christian meetings, reading the bible, singing Christian songs etc. Our dedication in this sense, is about us being

44

reserved *by* God and *for* God. Let's take a look at an example to make this clearer.

The Israelites were given clear instructions about how to live when they entered the Promise Land (see Deuteronomy 7). For one, they were told not to marry the inhabitants of the land, as this would lead them to abandon God and worship idols (see Deuteronomy 7:3-4). This was *everything* to do with knowing their *identity* as holy (set apart and dedicated to God):

*"For you are a people **holy** to the LORD your God. The LORD your God has chosen you to be a people for his treasured possession, out of all the peoples who are on the face of the earth. It was not because you were more in number than any other people that the LORD set his love on you and chose you, for you were the fewest of all peoples, but it is because the LORD loves you and is keeping the oath that he swore to your fathers, that the LORD has brought you out with a mighty hand and redeemed you from the house of slavery, from the hand of Pharaoh king of Egypt" (Deuteronomy 7:6-8).*

45

It's striking to see that the Israelites were told to observe these instructions *because* they *were* holy, not to *become* holy. Holiness is a definitive state that God's children *are*.

Not because of anything we've done to *achieve* holiness as an accolade, but because God has called us *out* from the world, for *His purposes* and to *reflect* His character. Why? Because when we reflect God's character in our day-to-day living, the world gets to experience a glimpse of God's goodness. This is what leads broken and hurting people to *want* to know the God of our Salvation (Romans 2:4).

Let's look at what Peter had to say to us:

"But you are a chosen race, a royal priesthood, a holy nation, a people for his own possession, that you may proclaim the excellencies of him who called you out of darkness into his marvellous light. Once you were not a people, but now you are God's people; once you had not

*received mercy, but now you have received mercy" (1
Peter 2:9-10).*

If holiness was defined by our actions rather than our
identity, then why would Peter rebuke the very same
"*royal priesthood and holy nation*" a few verses earlier
for *malice, deceit, hypocrisy, envy and slander?* (1 Peter
2:1) Peter didn't appeal to the reality of what these
disciples were *producing*, but he called them according
to their *God-nature*. He reminded them of *who* and
Whose they were.

This is perfectly in line with God's nature, calling those
things that are not as though they are (see Romans 4:17).

As a result of being set apart and embracing the restored
God nature, there will be a marked difference in our
behaviour compared to the world. Just as the Israelites
could be identified by their feasts and rituals, there will
be behaviours that show the world our God-like identity.
These behaviours should be an outer display of the work
God is doing in us (see Galatians 5:22-23).

47

Let's see what Peter said after talking about our set apart identity:

"Beloved, I urge you as sojourners and exiles to abstain from the passions of the flesh, which wage war against your soul. Keep your conduct among the Gentiles honourable, so that when they speak against you as evildoers, they may see your good deeds and glorify God on the day of visitation" (1 Peter 2:11-12).

This is just one example of how we should live differently as those set apart and distinctly different from the world. For further examples, see Ephesians 4:17-32, Ephesians 5, Ephesians 6, 2 Timothy 2:20-26, Romans 12:1-2, Romans 12:9-21. It's important that we don't lose sight of what we covered in the last chapter, but that we combine this with what we've learned so far about holiness.

Living out the call to walk in holiness does not cause us to *deserve* eternal life. This is a gift from God, extending His grace and mercy to mankind.

48

As a result of God's grace and mercy, we are empowered to live out our restored God-nature, walking in holiness. Our confidence comes from the *promise* that God would put *His* Spirit in us, give us new hearts, cause us to walk in His ways and obey His instructions (to stir up the faith to believe in this, take a look at the examples of: Ezekiel 36:22-32, Jeremiah 32:36-41, Jeremiah 31:31-34, Isaiah 59:20-21, Philippians 2:13). Even though we *believe* these promises and take *practical steps* to walk them out, our ability to obey is not something of ourselves. God initiated it. This is why we take no glory. It's all because of what *He* has done and produced in us.

Why is this so important?

Why is it so important for us to exercise the power God has given us to say no to sin, and yes to holiness? Ultimately, it's all about restoring the lost back to God. When we walk out our holy identity, this shows the world the nature of our Father (1 Peter 1:15-16). When that co-worker sabotages your work just to get ahead, your choice to not repay them with evil shows them God's graciousness. When that homeless man puts his hand out to ask for spare change, your generosity will show him God's kindness and undeserved love. When that person mistreats you and you decide to forgive them, that shows them God's mercy and unrelenting love. But if we choose to respond like the world, then why would the unbeliever *want* to join the Family of God?

Our holy identity is at the heart of God's mission to reconcile the lost back to Himself. We are representatives of our Father on Earth – ambassadors of God's family. In closing, let's take some time to reflect on the following verses:

"All this is from God, who through Christ reconciled us to himself and gave us the ministry of reconciliation; that is, in Christ God was reconciling the world to himself, not counting their trespasses against them, and entrusting to us the message of reconciliation. Therefore, we are ambassadors for Christ, God making his appeal through us. We implore you on behalf of Christ, be reconciled to God. For our sake he made him to be sin who knew no sin, so that in him we might become the righteousness of God" (2 Corinthians 5:18-21).

Reflection and application

1. What does Holiness mean to you after this
   chapter? How has this changed from what you
   thought before reading it?

   _____

   _____

   _____

   _____

   _____

   _____

   _____

   _____

2. Are there any former passions that you feel like
   you should start to move away from? If so, what
   are some steps you can take to start winning with
   this?

   _____

   _____

   _____

   _____

   _____

   _____

   _____

3. What are some practical ways that you can intentionally engage with God's grace to live a holy life?

_____

_____

_____

_____

_____

_____

_____

4. Looking at the fruit of the spirit described in
   Galatians 5:22-23, are there any particular traits
   you would you like to grow in? If so, which
   ones?

_____

_____

_____

_____

_____

_____

_____

Chapter 4 – Fit for purpose

So far, we've identified that the problem faced by
mankind is departing from living as those made in the
image of God. We've forsaken our God-nature. We've
also seen how God's gifts of grace and mercy create a
bridge for us to return to living out God's original
design. Additionally, we began to explore some of the
out-workings of the power that God has given us.

In particular, holiness, and how central it is to the
Christian journey and living a life worthy of our identity
and calling. Now that we've understood these truths, we
need to consider where exactly this leads us. Let's look
at the following verses:

*"In a wealthy home some utensils are made of gold and
silver, and some are made of wood and clay. The
expensive utensils are used for special occasions, and
the cheap ones are for everyday use. If you keep yourself
pure, you will be a special utensil for honourable use.
Your life will be clean, and you will be ready for the*

56

Master to use you for every good work" (2 Timothy 2:20-21 NLT).

One of the biggest frustrations that most of us face comes from the contrast between our lives and that of the early Church in Acts:

- The dead being raised to life (Acts (9:36-43);
- The lame being healed (Acts 3:1-10);
- Demons being cast out (Acts 16:16-18);
- A *literal* earthquake that opened prison doors after prisoners were praying and singing to God (Acts 16:25-26);
- Being able to live after shaking off a deadly snakebite (Acts 28:1-6);
- Sermons that cut to the heart, causing thousands to surrender to God, becoming a part of a devoted community of Christian brothers and sisters (Acts 2:14-47).

This is just a snapshot of some of the admirable experiences that we read about in the days of old. For many of us, our experience of Christianity is often very far from this.

Jesus said that signs like these, seen in the early church, would accompany believers (see Mark 16:17-18). He also said that we would not only do the works that He did, but also *greater* than these (John 14:12). So *why* has it seemed like such wishful thinking for us, the church, to walk out these truths?

While these signs and works aren't to be viewed as the end-game of Christianity, they aren't to be dismissed as "unrealistic" or "inapplicable to our time". Which brings us back to the question behind our frustration: *Why have we not been experiencing this?*

A call for intimacy

Something we repeatedly see about God through the scriptures is that He's always desired the deepest levels of intimacy with mankind. But He's never forced man to enter into this depth of relationship. He's always made the appeal for man to engage intimately and meaningfully with Him, but given man the right to decide the depth of his response to the appeal.

To sinful, rebellious man, God says, let's reason this one out. Though your sins are like scarlet and crimson red, I'll make them white as snow and wool. If you're willing and obedient to return back to intimacy with Me, you'll eat the good of the land. But if you choose to persist in your rebellion, you'll suffer the consequences of your decision (see Isaiah 1:18-20).

When God makes the appeal to mankind, man has two things he needs to consider:

1. The first is whether or not to surrender and come back home. Choosing to dethrone ourselves from internal majesty, no longer being our *own* god, but exalting Him as Lord and God over every fibre of our lives.

59

2. The second is this: *How close do you want to get and how deep do you want to go?*

The depth of intimacy God desires of us requires full, complete and undivided surrender. This is a high cost for man, but the resulting intimacy with God is immeasurably worth it. The closer we draw to God, the closer He'll draw to us (James 4:8). With increased levels of intimacy come greater depths of experiences as a child of God, greater exposure to more of Him, His nature, His passions and *His ways.*

The depth of our intimacy is up to us. We could choose a lightweight level of relational closeness to God; knowing Him from a distance, based on what we've *heard* from the teachings and experiences of others with Him (let's call this 'entry level intimacy'). Or we can pursue the greatest depths of relational closeness to God; knowing Him far more personally through our own experiences with Him, seeing Him with our very own eyes (let's call this 'mature intimacy') - see Job 42:5.

after the altar call | reasontobehold.com

Entry level intimacy is expected of a recent convert, one who hasn't spent much time or had much personal experience walking with God. They aren't to be regarded as less worthy or important in God's family, but as newly born babies in their formative stages. At this stage, they're starting to understand some of the fundamentals of their new God-nature, and the power they've been given to walk this out. They need to be taught by more experienced believers how to obey all that Jesus commanded – i.e. discipleship (see Matthew 28:19-20). It's not just telling the person to obey God, inviting them to church meetings and discipleship courses. But *true* discipleship is:

- Allowing the convert to walk with the teacher and see the God-nature lived out in practical, real-life settings. Jesus modelled this by inviting his disciples to follow Him and do life with Him. They were able to *see* Him practice love and forgiveness, gracefully asking the Father to forgive his persecutors (theory – Matthew 5:43-48, practice – Luke 23:34-38).

61

- Developing a close enough relationship with the convert to lovingly correct them when they're not living out the restored God-nature (see examples: Matthew 26:51-54/John 18:10-11, Luke 9:46-48).

As believers, we'll undoubtedly be faced with various trials, tests and situations in life. These will always challenge us to either live out our restored God-nature, or behave as those still enslaved to the old, sinful nature. This is why Jesus warned his us as His disciples that in this world we would have tribulation (John 16:33). It's also why Paul warned that all who desire to live a godly life would be persecuted (2 Timothy 2:12). The trials, tribulations and persecutions create opportunities to grow closer to God and become more acquainted with *His ways*. They test the strength of our faith and what we *really* believe about our identity (do we *believe* we have a restored God-nature, or are we still slaves to our old, sinful nature?).

Fire is used to purify gold, increasing its value through the removal of impurity. Equally, the various trials in our daily lives provide the fire that removes impurities. As we yield to our God-nature and *resist* our old and sinful nature, we become solid, immoveable and *mature* (see Ephesians 4:17-24). Maturity is what we were always called to (see Hebrews 6:1-3, 1 Corinthians 14:20), and yielding to our restored God-nature through the trials of life is one of the *key indicators of spiritual maturity*.

Mature intimacy is not reserved for the exclusive elite who are somehow at an unfair advantage because they were just *"born on the chest of God"*. Mature intimacy is available to *each and every one of us*. But remember, *we're* in control of how deep we go with God. If we want to be utensils of gold and silver, we have to be willing to endure the purifying process *through* the fiery trials. Alternatively, we can settle for being utensils of wood – useful from time to time in the hands of God, but not used for much more than the everyday matters. It's interesting to think about what happens when you put gold through fire compared to what happens when you put wood through fire. Fire purifies gold but incinerates wood. The fire increases the value of gold through

63

purification, but destroys the wood and reduces it to ashes. *So what do you think this means in the context of this chapter?*

If we desire to be vessels of gold – useful to God for special service, we *need* to have the right understanding of the various trials of life. If we're *scared and avoidant* of trials, or *refuse* to yield to our God-nature when the trials come, we'll be no more than the wood that is made for common use and *incinerated* by trials. As we choose to yield to our God-nature *daily* through trials, big and small, we'll come to experience and know God *far more intimately.* The more we *respond* to trials *according to our restored God-nature,* the more we *graduate* in maturity – no longer knowing God based on the theory we've heard, but from our own *intimate experiences of seeing Him for ourselves.* The more we grow in this intimacy, the more we become *special utensils* for God, experiencing *far* greater depth of life as His children. This is one of the key ways we come to *know* God and His ways *far* more intimately than if we'd stayed at entry level intimacy (2 Timothy 2:20-21). So the choice is yours to make: *How close do you want to get? How deep do you want to go?*

Reflection and application

1. What does intimacy with God look like to you?

_____

_____

_____

_____

_____

_____

_____

2. How do you feel about your current intimacy
   level with God?

_____

_____

_____

_____

_____

_____

_____

3. Is the concept of becoming closer to God
    something that excites you or slightly scares you?
    Why?

    _____

    _____

    _____

    _____

    _____

    _____

    _____

4. What are some day to day steps you can take to work on your intimacy with God?

_____

_____

_____

_____

_____

_____

_____

5. What are some impurities that you feel God is working with you to refine?

_____

_____

_____

_____

_____

_____

_____

6. Are there any trials in your life that could be used as opportunities for refinement?

_____

_____

_____

_____

_____

_____

Chapter 5 – Children of the King

When we become children of God, *everything* changes.
Literally, *everything*. We are a *new* creation, with *new*
habits, *new* values and a *new* God-nature (see 2
Corinthians 5:17). *Everything* about how we see life *has
to be different*. We were once blinded by the god of this
age, but our sight has been *restored* by the light of the
world! (see 2 Corinthians 4:4 and John 8:12). The
miracle of sight for a blind person *completely* changes
everything! It gives them the *confidence* to walk their
steps out *fearlessly*. Likewise, our adoption into God's
family as His children should cause a *dynamic,
noticeable shift* in the way we approach life. Let's take a
look from another angle.

Imagine being a beggar, born and raised in poverty.
You've never had much and only survived on the
passing generosity of others. One day, the king and his
convoy are passing through your city. As you see the
convoy approaching, you start waving your cardboard

72

sign, hoping to get their attention. The king gazes
through the tinted windows, and fixes his attention on
you. He focuses intently on your sign, making out the
words that it reads – "homeless and hungry, anything
helps". Consumed with compassion, he orders his driver
to pull over. In this brief moment, *everything* changes in
your world.

He steps out of the car, stretches out his hand and tells
you to come with him. With tears in your eyes, you take
his hand, rise to your feet and wrap your arms around
him. You've accepted his irresistible offer. You had no
idea *why* he chose to be so kind and generous, offering to
share his wealth and prosperity with you. But you *know*
this is an opportunity not to be questioned. So you leave
your cardboard sign and everything behind, and follow
him into his car. You sit with him in the backseat, *totally*
in awe, *totally* overwhelmed. The weight of the tears
suddenly become unbearable. You take a deep breath,
and begin to weep. He offers you a tissue and
reassuringly says:

"It's okay. You'll never go back to that life again. I'm taking you in as my son".

This represents what's happened to us as followers of Christ. God has adopted us as *His own* (see Galatians 4:4-7, Ephesians 1:3-6). Don't just read that last sentence and miss the depths of what this means. The *Sovereign Creator of the heavens and earth* has *adopted* you into *His* family. You're no longer a fatherless, hopeless beggar. You've been welcomed into *the* Royal family so *everything* about you and your life *has* changed. But *if* we *really* believed this was true, then wouldn't our lives reflect this? *Without a shadow of a doubt.* Let's take a look at a few examples.

Peter

Peter walked, talked and lived with Jesus. When Jesus said that all His disciples would scatter and forsake Him, Peter strongly resisted. Declaring his allegiance to Jesus, vowing to die if necessary to prove his loyalty (see Matthew 26:30-35). But when the rubber met the road,

74

he backed down, denying that he even *knew* Jesus (Matthew 26:69-75).

Compare this with Acts 4, where Peter was arrested and threatened, commanded to stop speaking and teaching about Jesus (see Acts 4:1-22). He wasn't moved by the threats, and with John, he boldly declared:

"...Whether it is right in the sight of God to listen to you rather than to God, you must judge, for we cannot but speak of what we have seen and heard" (Acts 4:19-20).

Paul

Writing from prison with no earthly certainty of the future, Paul was unmoved by circumstances that would cause most to faint and fear. He had *total* confidence in God and His *Sovereignty*. This is why Paul boldly declared:

"...Yes, and I will rejoice, for I know that through your prayers and the help of the Spirit of Jesus Christ this will

75

turn out for my deliverance, as it is my eager expectation and hope that I will not be at all ashamed, but that with full courage now as always Christ will be honored in my body, whether by life or by death. For to me to live is Christ, and to die is gain" (Philippians 1:18-21).

What about you and I?

As God's children, our response to difficult circumstances should be different from our unsaved friends and family. There are *countless* examples that show this through the scriptures. We should respond *confidently* when faced by challenging situations. When most are afraid, we should be at peace. It's *not* that we pretend to not see or feel the situation. We *acknowledge* what's in front of us. But what makes us different is that we recognise **God is Infinitely Bigger**. So we surrender what's in front of us to Him, *refuse* to walk defeated or weighed down by fear. But choosing to *walk* in our newly restored *God-nature*, we're *certain* that we can trust *totally* in God's Sovereignty.

David was faced by a *tremendous* enemy who had the Israelite army hopeless and afraid. Regardless, David stood *confident* in God. He *remembered* God's faithfulness in past situations (see 1 Samuel 17:34-37). Through his confidence in God, David triumphed over his enemy *against all odds.*

Abraham also stood confident in God, *far* beyond human understanding. God granted him and Sarah a child at an age of statistical impossibility. Despite this unnatural accomplishment of magnificence, Abraham took his miracle child and was ready to sacrifice him in obedience to God. Why? Because Abraham had *complete confidence* that his Father and God was able to resurrect his precious child from the dead (see Genesis 22:1-14 and Hebrews 11:17-19).

That's not realistic! Or *is* it?

I'm totally aware of how at times, our initial reaction to life situations can be fear and doubt. It feels easier to yield to our raw and unprocessed emotions. But this is only returning to our old and dead nature. Looking through the Psalms, we see the same David who slayed Goliath reacting with lamentation and despair. Here's an example:

"How long, O LORD? Will you forget me forever? How long will you hide your face from me? How long must I take counsel in my soul and have sorrow in my heart all the day? How long shall my enemy be exalted over me" *(Psalm 13:1-2).*

Whilst David's initial reactions expressed raw emotion and questioned how long God would forget him, he finished the Psalm by saying:

"But I have trusted in your steadfast love; my heart shall rejoice in your salvation. I will sing to the LORD, because he has dealt bountifully with me" *(Psalm 13:5-6).*

This is just one example of many where we can see that despite the fears and doubts that came with the situation,

David continually placed his hope and trust in God. Even his expressed raw emotions showed that his mind was fixed on God. He *did* express frustrations, but as we see here, he concluded with a *strong resolve.* The Sovereignty of God *prevailed* over his frustrations.

As God's children, we ought to stand confident in Him and His Sovereignty over *all* the circumstances of life. Assured that He'll work all things together for our good (see Romans 8:28), and that He'll never leave or forsake us (see Deuteronomy 31:6). This attitude is one of the things that sets us apart from those who don't trust God. This is a big part of our witness. Seeing the peace God gives us and how He comes through grabs the attention of our unsaved friends and family. It could be what shows them their *ultimate* need for salvation (see for example Acts 4:13 and Philippians 1:27-28). But living in peace in the face of fear is only possible by *walking in our newly restored God-nature.* So as we grow confident in our identity as God's children, we'll learn to stay centred and signpost others to God.

79

<u>Reflection and application</u>

1. How has your new identity as God's child affected your present life?

_____

_____

_____

_____

_____

_____

_____

2. Have you fully let go of your old identity, and embraced your new position in God's family? If not, why so?

_____

_____

_____

_____

_____

_____

_____

3. Difficulty, challenges and trials are experienced
    by all of us, regardless of our relationship with
    God (or lack thereof). How can your position in
    God's family influence your response to
    difficulties, challenges and trials?

_____

_____

_____

_____

_____

_____

4. Are there any challenging situations or
   circumstances in your life at the moment that you
   need to pour out to God about?

   _____

   _____

   _____

   _____

   _____

   _____

   _____

5. What are some practical steps you can take to stay anchored in God, even when things get difficult?

_____

_____

_____

_____

_____

_____

_____

Chapter 6 – The fight for spiritual sight

"There are two equal and opposite errors into which our race can fall about the devils. One is to disbelieve in their existence. The other is to believe, and to feel an excessive and unhealthy interest in them. They themselves [the devils] are equally pleased by both errors and hail a materialist or a magician with the same delight" – C.S. Lewis, The Screwtape Letters

We learnt in chapter two that the prison doors have been burst open for all believers, freeing us from the chains of sin. What we *didn't* explore was the person who is *extremely* frustrated by our freedom – *Satan*. The very accuser (Revelation 12:10) who *rejoiced* at our imprisonment, gnashed his teeth as he saw Jesus settle our sin-debt. He watched *powerlessly* as Christ stripped him of the authority he once had over us (Colossians 2:13-15).

Our enemy goes around like a *raging* lion, looking for a victim to consume (1 Peter 5:8). This doesn't mean we have to be scared of him, since he's already defeated (Luke 10:19, Colossians 2:13-15). I *can't* overemphasise this enough. All authority was given to Jesus Christ, our Lord, Shepherd and Saviour (Matthew 28:18). Jesus gave this authority to us, God's children. This goes from brand new converts to seasoned and mature Christians. We have authority over *all* the power of the enemy (Luke 10:19). Darkness *does* not and *cannot* overcome light (John 1:5). As children of light (1 Thessalonians 5:5), we *shine* in the darkness. We overcome it and change the atmosphere from darkness to light (Ephesians 5:8-14). *We* have no need to be afraid of Satan, wizards, witches, warlocks or anything from the kingdom of darkness. But we *do* have to stay constantly *aware* of Satan's cunning ways, knowing that he *preys* on the ignorant, the unsuspecting and the naïve (see 1 Peter 5:8, 2 Corinthians 2:11). Those, he may devour.

If we want to be victorious, we *can't* afford to walk through life relying only on our five senses. God is Spirit (John 4:24). As His children, made in His image and walking in the restored God-nature, we need to *engage* with the spiritual.

Fighting an enemy we can't physically see

As Christians, we're fighting an enemy we can't *see* with our natural eyes. Because of this, we need to study and understand his weapons and strategies. Otherwise, we can easily walk blindly into a spiritual ambush. Our enemy is constantly seeking to sift us like wheat (Luke 22:31), so what we don't know about him can really hurt us (Hosea 4:6). Our ignorance of his cunning strategies gives him a huge advantage over us (see 2 Corinthians 2:11). Our war is spiritual and not fought according to the natural things of this world (2 Corinthians 10:4-6). Our battle is against rulers, authorities, cosmic powers and spiritual forces of evil (Ephesians 6:12).

A key part of the restored God-nature is the *mind*. We have now been given access to the mind of Christ, which is the very mind of God (see 1 Corinthians 2:16, Colossians 1:15). According to this mind, we now have the ability to go beyond our limited, natural understanding and interpretations of life. We can now see things from heavens perspective. This is essentially the gift of **spiritual sight**.

When the scripture states that we're now seated with Christ in heavenly places (Ephesians 2:6), this reveals not just a positional change of intimacy and righteousness, but also a change in *perspective*. Our viewpoint no longer has to be horizontal, based on our earthly senses and position. Just like John, we've been invited to come up higher so that we can *see* things clearly from heaven's point of view (see Revelation 4:1). Among many other advantages, this new perspective enables us to *see* our enemy and stay alert to his underhanded tactics.

The cost of not seeing from heaven's perspective

Whilst we've been granted *access* to the mind of Christ (the ability to tap into His way of thinking), we have to *choose* to make use of this. Remember, we were blinded for years before our conversion (2 Corinthians 4:4). In all that time, we became accustomed to seeing life through our natural senses, responding and reacting to things with no spiritual discernment (see 1 Corinthians 2:14). Having spent so long interpreting life through these broken lenses, it's easy to bring this broken practice into our new life with God. So it's extremely important that we're *active* about *changing the way we think*. One of the ways we can do this is by regularly reading and practicing living out God's Word. By doing so, our thinking and our lives are directed by the very mind of Christ (see Romans 12:2, Psalm 110:105). It keeps us from walking blind as we once were. It equips us to navigate life with **spiritual sight**.

*"Now this I say and testify in the Lord, that you must no longer walk as the Gentiles do, in the **futility of their minds**. They are darkened in their understanding, alienated from the life of God because of the ignorance that is in them, due to their hardness of heart. They have become callous and have given themselves up to sensuality, greedy to practice every kind of impurity. But*

*that is not the way you learned Christ!— assuming that you have heard about him and were taught in him, as the truth is in Jesus, to **put off your old self, which belongs to your former manner of life** and is corrupt through deceitful desires, and to **be renewed in the spirit of your minds**, and to **put on the new self, created after the likeness of God in true righteousness and holiness**"* – Ephesians 4:17-24

We saw earlier that living the restored God-nature requires intentional input from us. Similarly, we have a part to play in *developing* our spiritual sight. We need to *know* God's Word and *choose* to live by its principles. We have to make *conscious,* daily decisions to let our lives be directed by His Word. Not our emotions, not our assumptions and not the popular opinions of this world (see Proverbs 3:5-6 and Romans 12:2). We can't afford to settle for anything less than Heaven's perspective. When we apply God's Word and let it direct our decisions, it acts as the torch we need to see in this darkened world (Psalm 119:105, Psalm 119:130). But when we refuse to use this torch provided by God, the

91

consequences are vast and significant. Let's explore one example of what this looks like in practice.

Dealing with mistreatment and offence

As our battle is spiritual, we can't physically *see* the traps of the enemy. So our instinctive response to mistreatment will often be resentment, unforgiveness and speaking negatively about our offender. They're automatically seen as the enemy at hand. Because of this, we may turn on them and stop walking in unity.

Unresolved offence leads to a subtle root of unforgiveness. We're so caught up in our emotions and pride that we completely fail to see Satan's influence in our affairs. Our enemy is *extremely* opportunistic; he'll happily whisper ungodly thoughts *related* to the mistreatment. He's constantly searching for *any* opportunity to divide (see 1 Peter 5:8, 2 Corinthians 2:5-11 and Ephesians 4:26-27). He's equally concerned with keeping our non-Christian loved ones blinded from the gospel (see 2 Corinthians 4:3-4). So when we demonise our offenders and start to see *them* as the enemy, we fall prey to Satan's trap and help him achieve his goals. But we're only able to see these sneaky little traps when looking from *Heaven's* perspective. When we shine God's Word on our situation, all hidden things become clear. Identifying Satan's agenda in the midst of mistreatment is *key* to walking out the restored God-nature.

As God's children, we *already* have much work to do. More work than there are workers (Matthew 9:36-38). So we can't afford to write each other off as though we don't *need* one another. We're all uniquely important and valuable, playing a key part in God's Kingdom (see 1 Corinthians 12:12-26). When we fall into Satan's trap of offence, the body of Christ suffers great harm. Unresolved issues become blockers to working well together. As the offence grows deeper, it becomes bitterness. We constantly replay the offence in our minds and our "sharing" becomes unhelpful gossip. This further damages the body of Christ as the same ungodly attitude is spread amongst others (see Hebrews 12:14-15).

When we live like this, we misrepresent Jesus to the world. They think: *"If he/she follows Jesus and that's how they behave, then I don't want anything to do with Christianity"*. Think about it; God makes His appeal to the world *through* us, His children and ambassadors (see 2 Corinthians 5:17-20). We're the flagship 'product' from His Kingdom, the experience people have of us will either draw them to God or push them away. The credibility of our gospel message relies heavily on our unity with God *and* one another (see John 17:20-21 and John 13:35). When we don't show the world the better way to deal with mistreatment, our gospel presentation loses its appeal.

We can't forget the mission Jesus left us. We're called to preach the gospel and disciple people (see Mark 16:15 and Matthew 28:19-20). The words we preach carry the most weight when our actions support them. So we can't just *speak* about God's mercy, grace and forgiveness.

94

We must *show* these great gifts to others. Our priority shouldn't be getting our way and winning the present disagreement; it should be the same as our Father's – *offering salvation and forgiveness.*

This is an attitude that's developed by *reading, understanding and applying* God's Word, changing the way that we think (see Romans 12:1-2). We stop responding based purely on our natural senses and are better in tune with what's *really* going on. We see Satan's agenda in the midst of the mistreatment. We fight with all we have to keep us united. Sometimes we're successful and the relationship is restored. Other times, we've tried our best to resolve things, but the other party isn't so willing (see Romans 12:18).

Fighting for spiritual sight...

We mentioned before that God's word is the torch that helps us to see things *clearly* (see Psalm 119:105). This can't be stressed enough. It's *really* important that we take time to read and study The Word. Through this, we

95

not only learn about Satan's strategies (2 Corinthians 2:11), but also how to use our new nature to defeat them (2 Corinthians 5:17, Ephesians 4:17-24). All that we've learnt throughout this book has come from God's Word. It's been a lamp to our feet, giving us understanding on how to live after the alter call. This shows us how *essential* God's word is in the process of us developing and exercising spiritual sight.

As well as a light to our path, God's Word is the very weapon that equips us for our unseen battle. Consider the following:

*"Finally, **be strong in the Lord** and **in the strength of his might. Put on the whole armor of God, that you may be able to stand against the schemes of the devil.** For we do not wrestle against flesh and blood, but against the rulers, against the authorities, against the cosmic powers over this present darkness, against the spiritual forces of evil in the heavenly places. **Therefore take up the whole armor of God, that you may be able to withstand in the evil day, and having done all, to***

96

*stand firm. Stand therefore, having fastened on **the belt of truth**, and having put on **the breastplate of righteousness**, and, as shoes for your feet, having put on **the readiness given by the gospel of peace**. In all circumstances take up the **shield of faith**, with which you can extinguish all the flaming darts of the evil one; and take **the helmet of salvation**, and <u>**the sword of the Spirit, which is the word of God**</u>, praying at all times in the Spirit, with all prayer and supplication..."* – Ephesians 6:10-18

These verses make it clear that there's an unseen war going on. The only way to prepare and gain victory is by equipping ourselves with the *full* armour of God. Much can be said about each part of this armour, but let's focus on the sword of the Spirit - *God's Word*. We don't use swords anymore, so it's easy to miss what's being said here. In modern terms, God's word is like a combination of guns, tanks, sniper rifles and grenades. It enables us to defend against enemy attacks, and to take back the territory which he previously stole. Life without the full armour of God is like walking blindfolded into battle with our hands tied behind our backs.

God's word teaches, corrects and equips us for our spiritual battle (2 Timothy 3:16-17). By reading, studying and meditating on it, we're exposed to more and more of the restored God-nature. It helps us understand how to successfully navigate life in our new identity (see Joshua 1:8).

The Word also acts as a mirror, exposing our blind spots and blemishes (see James 1:22-25 and Hebrews 4:12-13). But it's not enough to just *know* about them. We need to take *action* to correct what we've seen (see James 1:22-25). Renewing our minds daily, choosing to walk in love, after the very likeness of God (see Ephesians 4:1, Colossians 1:10 and Ephesians 4:17-24).

Reflection and application

1. What are some of the advantages of us being *consciously aware* that we have an enemy (satan) whose ultimate goal is our downfall?

_____

_____

_____

_____

_____

_____

2. What are some likely outcomes if we bury our
   heads in the sand and ignore satan's existence
   and agenda against us individually, and as the
   wider body of Christ?

   _____

   _____

   _____

   _____

   _____

   _____

   _____

   _____

3. What are some likely outcomes if we fall into the
   opposite error of over-focusing on satan?

_____

_____

_____

_____

_____

_____

_____

4. How do you deal with mistreatment and offence?
   Have you been able to identify satan's agenda in
   it all?

---

5. Are there any particular people you were
   reminded of when reading about offence and
   mistreatment? If so, how will you respond based
   on what we've covered in this chapter?

   _____

   _____

   _____

   _____

   _____

   _____

   _____

Chapter 7 – Bringing it all together

We've been on this journey and learnt some really cool concepts – some new to us, some familiar. But what we really need to do now is *apply* the truths we've covered. One of the mistakes we make is *constantly* searching for *new* information before we've put into practice what we already know.

Head knowledge alone can easily lead to arrogance and pride, which God actively opposes (see 1 Corinthians 8:1b and James 4:6). But when we *humbly* receive and *act* on His Word, we'll be blessed in all that we do (see James 1:21-25). There's a strength that comes from this. The Word prepares us to navigate life more effectively and enables us to endure the various storms that may come (Matthew 7:24-27). Let's recap some of the key truths covered and consider practical steps to apply them to our lives.

Chapter 1: Made in the image of God

God created man using the blueprint of Himself (Genesis
1:26-28). As His children and earthly representatives, we
were made with the very nature of God. He designed us
to reflect His attributes and ways, expressing this
throughout the earth. This was never about empty
religious devotion, but relationship and a way of life.
God wants His nature to permeate *all* areas of our lives.
He wants us to demonstrate His attributes and ways in
whatever we do.

Like Adam and Eve, we've all rebelled against God's
created order. Rather than reflecting God's nature in all
areas of life, we've devised our own way of doing things
(Romans 3:23). We've departed from our God-like
identity, adopting the sinful nature of Satan.

Chapter 2: A bridge for the chasm

The rebellion of man came at a price that none of us
could ever pay. It led to our enslavement to sin (Romans

6:16) and put us on a highway to eternal punishment
(Romans 6:23, John 3:16-21, 2 Thessalonians 1:9-10).
Jesus came to rescue us from our slavery to sin and the
punishment due for our rebellion (see Titus 2:14, John
3:36, John 8:24, 1 John 4:10).

The gravity of Jesus' sacrifice goes far deeper than is
often portrayed. We could *never* do anything to satisfy
the righteous requirements of God's standards (see
Romans 8:3-4, Romans 3:20, 2 Corinthians 5:21). So our
salvation was a miraculous, undeserved gift in itself. But
beyond the great gift of heaven after death, we've been
given the power to say *no* to our old nature. This was
once *impossible*! We are a *new* creation as a result of
Christ's sacrifice. We've been given a *new* identity and a
new nature (2 Corinthians 5:17). This is a miraculous
restoration of the God-nature we were given at the
beginning of all creation (see Genesis 1:26-27).

Chapter 3: Be holy, for He is holy

The restored God-nature doesn't work on autopilot, but requires *intentional* input from us. Faith without works is dead, and beliefs with no supporting actions achieve nothing (see James 2:14-26). God is the One who empowers us to walk out the restored God-nature (see Ezekiel 36:22-27, Philippians 2:12-13). But we have to go from just saying we believe this, to walking it out in our daily living.

We walk out our restored God-nature by resisting the devil and the passions of our old sinful nature. We choose instead to submit to God through ***intentional obedience*** to His standards (James 4:8, 1 Peter 1:14-16). This is not a matter of trying to *earn* God's approval and eternal life (since this is a free gift we can't earn - Ephesians 2:8-10, Romans 3:20). But it *is* a matter of walking out the restored God-nature, living out the identity that was birthed in us at our conversion.

107

At the core of this restored God-nature is our holiness (being set apart and different from what is common because of our dedication to God). Holiness isn't defined by our actions, rather, it's our very identity. Our godly conduct (motivated by love) is an outward evidence of our distinct differences from the world because of our dedication to God.

Chapter 4: Fit for purpose

What we believe about our restored God-nature will undoubtedly be put to the test. We'll be faced with various trials, tests and situations that will call for us to make a decision: live out our newly restored identity or live out our old sinful nature. The fiery trials, tests and situations give us the opportunity to grow closer to God and learn *His ways*.

Fire is used to purify gold, increasing its value through the removal of impurity. Equally, various trials provide the fire that purifies us as we yield to God and *resist* our old nature (see Ephesians 4:17-24). By yielding to God, we become solid, immoveable and *mature*. This is what we've been called to - *maturity* (see Hebrews 6:1-3, 1 Corinthians 14:20). Consistently yielding to our restored God-nature through trials is a *key indicator* of spiritual maturity.

We're in control of how deep we go with God. If we want to be utensils of gold and silver (see 2 Timothy 2:20-21), we have to be willing to endure the trials. Alternatively, we can settle for a much lesser experience by being utensils of wood – useful from time to time in the hands of God, but not used for much more than the everyday matters.

If we desire to be vessels of gold – useful to God for special service and depth of experience, we *need* to have the right understanding of trials. If we're *scared and avoid* trials, or *refuse* to yield to God, we're no more than wood, suitable for common use. As we yield to God *daily*, we'll come to experience and know Him *far more intimately*. We grow in maturity, knowing God not based on theory alone, but from our own intimate experiences -

seeing Him for ourselves. The more we grow in
intimacy, the more we become *special utensils* for God,
experiencing *far* greater depth of life as His child.

Chapter 5: Children of the King

As God's children, we're a *new* creation, with *new*
habits, *new* values and a *new* God-nature (see 2
Corinthians 5:17). Everything about how we see life *has
to be different.* We were once blinded by the god of this
age, but our sight has been *restored* by the light of the
world! (see 2 Corinthians 4:4 and John 8:12). The
miracle of sight for a blind person *completely* changes
everything! It gives them *confidence* to walk their steps
out *fearlessly.* Likewise, our adoption into God's family
should cause a *dynamic, noticeable shift* in the way we
approach *all* areas of life.

As children of the *Sovereign Creator, King and Ruler of
all*, we should respond *confidently* when faced by
situations that cause most to tremble and fear. It's not
that we don't see or feel. We *acknowledge* what's in

110

front of us, but we *surrender it to God*. We confidently *trust* that *He* is *Infinitely Bigger*. We *refuse* to walk defeated, weighed down by fear and our *old* nature. But we *walk* in our new identity, *certain* that we can trust *totally* in God's sovereignty. This produces a distinct courage and boldness (see Proverbs 28:1).

When people see our courage and boldness in tough situations, *this* could be what turns their attention to God (see for example Acts 4:13 and Philippians 1:27-28). If we let our old nature dictate our actions, then we'll look no different.

Chapter 6: The fight for spiritual sight

We have an enemy who wants to destroy us. We don't have to be afraid of him, since he's already defeated. But we *do* have to stay constantly *aware* of his cunning ways, knowing that he *relishes* on the ignorant, the unsuspecting and the naïve.

We now have access to the mind of Christ, which is the very mind of God. We now have spiritual sight. We're now able to go beyond our limited, natural understanding and interpretations of life. We can see things for what they *truly* are from heavens perspective.

Our spiritual sight needs to be developed and exercised. We do this through reading, studying and meditating on The Word. Once we *know* The Word, we need to *do* it.

God's Word is also a crystal clear mirror, exposing our blind spots. It *shows* us the ugly truth about the areas we've not yet surrendered to God, and provides us with a reminder of our new identity. But a mirror is useless if we don't *adjust* our appearance based on what it shows us. Similarly, when we *see* the blemishes revealed by The Word, we *need* to take action to correct them.

Concluding comments

Thank you for journeying with us through this book and for recognising that there's more to life after the alter call. If the journey provoked questions and thoughts within you, that's not bad at all! My prayer is that you'll journey with the Holy Spirit to search out the scriptures and get answers to these questions. Don't forget to utilise the community of believers around you too!

Lastly, I pray that you walk away from this book *confident* in the life-changing transformation that took place at your conversion. May you walk *fully assured* that you *are* a new creation in Christ (2 Corinthians 5:17). As a new creation, God restored in you the very God-nature that man once had in the Garden of Eden (see Genesis 1:26-27). You are God's child and representative here on earth. Go forth with this newly restored nature and identity, reproduce it by introducing others to Christ and impact your world by expressing the nature and character of God to everyone you meet.

God bless you richly!

Reflection and application

1. What are some of the biggest practical lessons
   you've taken away from this book?

   _____

   _____

   _____

   _____

   _____

   _____

   _____

2. What decisions do you need to make today in order to grow in your reflection of God's nature and to better walk out your new identity?

_____

_____

_____

_____

_____

_____

_____

3. What key scriptures can you chew on and pray in order to help you win with the decisions you're making?

_____

_____

_____

_____

_____

_____

_____

4. If you were sat in a room face-to-face with God
    right now, what would you ask him to help you
    with based on the thoughts provoked in your
    mind whilst reading this book? (why not pour out
    to God in prayer about these things?)

    _____

    _____

    _____

    _____

    _____

    _____

    _____

Printed in Great Britain
by Amazon